Contents

1: True Lo♥e
2: A Kiss 💋
3: Breakfast at The Lillipad Café
4: The Outer Limits
5: A Troubled Man
6: The Punisher
7: The Non-Thinker
8: The Thinking of Privilege
9: No Expectations
10: Thick as a Brick
(Testa Dura)
11: Fickle Friend
12: Bad Medicine
13: Let it Flow
14: Que Sera Sera
(What Will Be, Will Be)
15: Whatever Works for You
16: On the Edge of Forever
17: What is Growing in Your Garden?
18: I'm Stupid
19: I Will Not Let You Down
20: The Garden of Earthly Delights
(Il Giardino delle Delizie Terrene)
21: Ownership
(Possession)
22: Brain-Dead
(Morte Cerebrale)
23: Objectification
(Dehumanisation)
24: I am an Individual
(Sono un Individuo)
25: The Devil's Hand
(La Mano del Diavolo)
26: Lo♥e is......
(L'amore è......)
27: Don't Be So Precious
(Non Essere Così Prezioso)

Contents

28: Imagine
29: Terrific
30: Relationships
31: Treaty
32: Live in the Moment
(Vivi nel Momento)
33: Things People Say That Irritate Me
(Cose che le Persone Dicono che mi Irritano)
34: Dog My Cat
35: I Lo♥e You
(but I'm Not "In Lo♥e" with You)
36: It ALL Works Out in the End!
(Alla Fine Funziona Tutto!)
37: The Demon Hunter
38: We All Wear a Mask
(Tutti Indossiamo una Maschera)
39: You Choose Your Own Emotions
(Tu Scegliere le tue Emozioni)
40: The triumph of IDIOCY & STUPIDITY!
41: The Best Laid Plans of Mice & Men
(I Migliori Piani di Topi e Uomini)
42: False Gods
(Falsi Dei)
43: The Human Academy
(L'Accademia Umana)
44: Personas
45: Guys Just Want to Fuck
(I Ragazzi Vogliono Solo Scopare)
46: Toy Boy
47: Ego IS a Dirty Word
(L'ego è una Parolaccia)
48: The Girl from Ipanema Returns
(Vuelve la Chica de Ipanema)
49: Eat My Pussy
(Mangia la Mia Figa)
50: It's Not About What I want
(Non si Tratta di Quello che Voglio)

True Love

Tainted Love.
Everlasting Love.
Sinful Love.
Lustful Love.
Hateful Love.
Unrequited Love.
Immoral Love.
Wrong Love.
Sexy Love.
Female Love.
Male Love.
Godly Love.
Devil Love.
Ungreatful Love.
Brotherly Love.
Sisterly Love.
Motherly Love.
Brutal Love.
Tough Love.
Forever Love.
Baby Love.
Sacrificial Love.
Spiritual Love.
Psychedelic Love.
Consumer Love.
Bottled up Love.
Bottled Love.
Soul Love.
Deep Love.
Rarified Love.
No Love.
True Love.

There is no "true" Love!

"The Don"
25.07.2020

A Kiss

What is a kiss, but 2 lips pressed together?
But it is much more than that.

I kiss the sky.
I kiss the Earth.
I kiss the Moon.
I kiss the stars.
I kiss the wind.
I kiss the Sun.
I kiss the raindrops.
I kiss the rainbow.
I kiss the rose.
I kiss the parsley.
I kiss the basil.
I kiss the night.
I kiss the day.
I kiss the moonlight.
I kiss the shadows.

I kiss your beauty.
I kiss your forehead.
I kiss your nose.
I kiss your cheeks.
I kiss your lips.
I kiss your neck.
I kiss your breasts.
I kiss your belly.
I kiss your pussy.
I kiss your inner thighs.
I kiss your toes.

I kiss your mind.
I kiss your he♥rt.
I kiss your soul.
I kiss your being.
I kiss your kindness.
I kiss your caring.
I kiss your compassion.
I kiss your energy.
I kiss your creativity.
I kiss your Lo♥e.
I kiss your life.

I kiss is not a kiss.
A smile is not a smile.

"The Don"
26.07.2020

Breakfast at The Lillipad Café

*"Walk right in.
Sit right down.
Baby, let your mind slow down.
Walk right in.
Sit right down.
Baby, let your mind roll on."*

Welcome!
Come right in.
"Oka", the *"Black Queen of Glebe"*.
Greets you with a smile.
She's from FNQ.
She's First Nations Peoples.
And she's *"rigidig"*.
She's the *"real deal"*.
Her laugh is infectious.
Her laugh is contagious.
She'll make you the best coffee you've ever had in your life.

Then there is *"The Jimmy"*.
She can do anything.
Because she knows everything.
She's a *"Jimmy"* of all trades.
With the most beautiful smile ever.

"Onya Monya" is the sweetest person I've ever met.
She follows the *"Sydney Roosters"* rugby league club.
She's in Lo♥e with *"Teddy Tredesco"*, but who isn't?

Then there's "Lori Cartier".
She's a "Jewel in the Crown".
Just here name suggests.
She only works on Sundays.
I wish she worked every day.
Her beauty is iridescent.

In the kitchen there's *"Lazio"*.
Truly a magician with food.
His food is so delicious.
You think you've just had your very last meal.
You'll be coming back for more.
That's for sure.
With his little helper *"Carlos"*,
They are the dynamic duo.

Then there are the regulars, that I only know of.
But there are so many more.
Who would never go anywhere else!
There's *"Thirsty Kirsty"*.
There's *"Sue shhhhhhhhh"*.
There's *"Isabel"*.
There's *"Sue SU"*.
There's *"JJ"*.
There's the *"crew from the local primary school"*.

The menu is to die for.
They incorporate *"Indigenous plants"* into their dishes.
Such as *"Davidson Plum"*, *"Wattleseed"* & *"GrunTea Nettle"*.
They are not scared to think "outside the plate".
Here is just a sample.
Vegan or regular, the choice is yours.
The go dish *"poached eggs with hollandaise sauce"*.
The *"Vegan"* omelette.
To die for!
The *"Turkish Breakfast"*, a platter made for 2.
There are so many more mouth-watering dishes.
"Gangurru Burger" with *"wattleseed"*, *"pepperleaf"* & *"saltbush spiced kangaroo patty"*.
"Native Flora", house-made patty with *"saltbush"*, *"wattleseed"* & *"pepperleaf"*.
Too many others to mention here.

So, if you're ever in old Glebe town.
Why not come around.
"Walk right in."
You'll be welcome anytime.
What a way to start your day.
With breakfast at *"The Lillipad Café"*!

"The Don"
27.07.2020

The Outer Limits

What have you seen?
What have you heard?
What have you felt?
What have you sensed?

Have you ever been scared?
Have you ever been frightened?
Have you ever been terrified?
Have you ever been horrified?

Have you ever wanted to know what's on the *"other side"*?
Have you ever wanted to know what's on the *"inside"*?
Have you ever wanted to know what's on the *"edge"*?
Have you ever wanted to know what's on *"The Outer Limits"*?

Maybe you should take a friend with you.
Someone who will have your back.
Someone who will stand their ground.
Someone who will not let you fall.

What's on the other side?
Are you up for it?
Are you ready for it?
Are you ready to step into *"The Outer Limits"*?

You have to be prepared that you may never come back.
Are you ready for that?
It's a *"one-way"* trip.
There's no coming back.

Once you have crossed over the threshold.
Once you have entered "The Outer Limits".
You may return.
But you won't *EVER* be the same.

You will never be the same again.
You will be changed forever.
You will be a different person.
Maybe, not even a person anymore.

Who knows?
Once you been to "The Outer Limits".

"The Don"
27.07.2020

A Troubled Man

He's got schemes.
He's got dreams.
He's got ideas.
He's got plans.
He's got thoughts.
He's got feelings.
He's got pain.
He's got suffering.
He's got nightmares.
He's got fears.
He's got hopes.
He's got high hopes.
He's got expectations.
He's got worries.
He's got problems.
He's got indigestion.
He's got constipation.
He's got heart problems.
He's got high blood pressure.
He's got weight issues.
He's got weighty issues.
He's got breathing problems.
He's got sleeping problems.
He's got women problems.
He's got money problems.
He's got children problems.
He's got gambling problems.
He's got trouble on his mind.

He's a troubled man.

"The Don"
27.07.2020

The Punisher

She doesn't drink.
She doesn't do drugs.
She doesn't fuck.
She doesn't do Lo♥e.

She has no mind.
Is that unkind?
She has no interests.
She only does Hate.

She lives by herself.
She has no friends.
She has no life.
She wants to be a wife.

She can't cook.
She can't sew.
She can't Lo♥e.
She can't fuck.

She wants to live the high life.
She wants to be rich.
She wants to be Lo♥ed.
She wants to be married.

She doesn't put out.
She doesn't give.
She doesn't Lo♥e.
She doesn't fuck.

She's melodramatic.
She's a *"drama queen"*.
She's very selfish.
She's very mean.

She's very quick to turn on you.
She's very quick to drop you like a "hot potato".
She's very quick to stop being your friend.
She's *"The Punisher"*.

"The Don"
28.07.2020

The Non-Thinker

(The Philosophers' Song)

Thinking causes problems & that is a fact.
We just have to Look at these great thinkers of history to know that.

"*Immanuel Kant* was a real pissant.
Who was very rarely stable.

Heidegger, Heidegger was a boozy beggar.
Who could think you under the table.

David Hume could out-consume
Wilhelm Freidrich Hegel.

And *Wittgenstein* was a beery swine.
Who was just as schloshed as *Schlegel*.

There's nothing *Nietzsche* couldn't teach ya.
'bout the raising of the wrist.
Socrates, himself, was permanently pissed.

John Stuart Mill, of his own free will.
On half a pint of shandy was particularly ill.

Plato, they say, could stick it away'
Half a crate of whiskey every day.

Aristotle, Aristotle was a bugger for the bottle.
And *Hobbes* was fond of his dram.

And *Rene Descartes* was a drunken fart.
"I drink, therefore I am."

Yes, *Socrates* himself is particularly missed.
A lovely little thinker, but a bugger when he's pissed."

("Bruce's Philosophers Song" by Monty Python)

Very unstable individuals.
So, please "*DON'T THINK*!"

"The Don"
28.07.2020

The Thinking Of Privilege

You think that you're better than everyone else.
You think that you can do whatever you please.
You think that you're "Special".
You think that you're "above" others.
You think that the rules don't apply to you.
You think that the laws are not there for you.
You think that you can come & go as you please.
You think that you can laugh at others that follow the rules.

You think that you're so clever.
You think that you're a rebel.
You think that you're a radical.
You think that you're a "free thinker".
You think that you're an "anarchist".
You think that you're "better" than all the rest.
You think that you're "smarter" than everyone.
You think that you are "entitled".
You think that you're "privileged".

But in fact, you are "elitist".
You are arrogant.
You are selfish.
You are conceited.
You are a hypocrite.
You are a "Fascist".

"The Don"
28.07.2020

No Expectations

It's all about *"Power"*.
It's all about making *"Demands"*.
It's all about having *"Expectations"*.
It's all about *"manipulation"*.
It's all about *"forcing"*.
It's all about *"holding on"*.
It's all about *"getting your own way"*.
It's all about *"Fear"*.

It's hard to *"let go"*.
It's hard to just *"go with the flow"*.
It's hard to just *"live in the moment"*.
It's hard to just let someone *"be"*.
It's hard to just let someone be *"free"*.
It's hard to just let go of your *"fears"*.

Fear of rejection.
Fear of loneliness.
Fear of abandonment.
Fear of failure.
Fear of loss of youth.
Fear of getting old.
Fear of old age.
Fear of not being wanted anymore.
Fear of not being Lo❤ed.
Fear of never being fucked ever again.

There's a knot in your stomach.
There's pain in your he❤rt.
There's a longing in your groin.
There's a voice in head saying;
"don't let it go!
You must push on.
You must not let go.
You must let them go.
You must pursue it until it's DEAD."

DON'T listen to that voice in your head.
DON'T listen to that voice, it's FEAR talking.
DON'T listen to that voice that tells you to Destroy.
DON'T listen to that voice & be strong.

Get rid of your *demands*.
Get rid of your *expectations*.
Get rid of your need for *POWER*.
Get rid of your need for *CONTROL*.

Have *NO* expectations!

"The Don"
28.07.2020

Thick as a Brick

(Testa Dura)

Don't you get it?
How many times do you have to be told?
You've got a *"hard"* head.
Just keep making the same mistakes.
Over & over & over again.
When will you ever learn?
Never, I guess.
'Cause you've got a *"testa dura"*.
You'll never learn.
Are you an *"idiot"* or something?
Maybe, you're *"Thick as a Brick"*?
Maybe when you're Dead.

You heard it all before.
But you're as *"weak as piss"*.
You just can't help yourself.
You just can't control yourself.
You've got to do it.
No matter how many times you tell yourself not to.
You just can't do it.
You give in to your baser instincts.
It must be a *"survival"* thing?

I guess it's just Fear that makes you do it.
Fear of Rejection.
It's a powerful emotion that's for sure.
Beats the *"Intellect"* every time.
When it's *"The Emotions"* vs *"The Intellect"*.
The *"Intellect"* is thrown out the window.
"The Emotions" rule supreme.
The *"He♥rt"* gets what the *"He♥rt"* wants.
But that's a delusion.
It's a trap.
It's a *"fool's errand"*.
It's a mistake.

Let your *"He ♥ rt"* go.
Let the *"noise"* in your head out.
You know what to do.
You've been here so many times before.
This is not new.
You've just gotta be strong.
Don't give in.
Keep your nerve.
Keep repeating to yourself,
"I can do this!
I can do this!
I can do this!"

"Time heals all wounds!"
That is so true.
So, don't be a *"testa dura"*.
Don't be *"Thick as a Brick"*!

Thick as a Brick

"The Don"
29.07.2020

Fickle Friend

Were you really my friend?
I don't think so.
Friendship doesn't seem to be very important to you.
In fact, I don't think you know what it means to be a friend.
You are one fickle friend!

You "talk the talk, but you don't walk the walk!"
You are quick to dump someone at the "drop of a dime".
You say you want to have friends.
But that is a lie!
You're way to selfish to be a "good" friend.
You are one fickle friend!

You dropped me as a friend because I said that I couldn't keep paying anymore.
"I don't feel good going for coffee with you.
I will stop hanging round you.
I don't want friends.
I don't need anyone have good life.
I have my own plans.
I done with people making me like I'm nothing."
This is your txt message.
I didn't bother to respond to such an absurd message.
I didn't want to dignify it with one.
You are one fickle friend!

It doesn't really worry me.
It's your loss.
I was the "best" friend you ever had.
And that is the "truth".
If you're ever really "honest" with yourself.
When you find yourself all alone.
In your one bedroom apartment.
In the cold & dark of the night.
Maybe you'll think about it.
And how a you are one fickle friend!

In the words of "Bob Dylan".
Who says it much more eloquently than me....
"You've got a lotta nerve to say you are my friend
When I was down you just stood there grinnin'
You've got a lotta nerve to say you got a helping hand to lend
You just want to be on the side that's winnin'

You say I let you down, ya know it's not like that
If you're so hurt, why then don't you show it?
You say you've lost your faith, but that's not where it's at
You have no faith to lose, and ya know it

I know the reason, that you talked behind my back
I used to be among the crowd you're in with
Do you take me for such a fool, to think I'd make contact
With the one who tries to hide what he don't know to begin with?

You see me on the street, you always act surprised
You say "how are you?", "good luck", but ya don't mean it
When you know as well as me, you'd rather see me paralyzed
Why don't you just come out once and scream it

No, I do not feel that good when I see the heartbreaks you embrace
If I was a master thief, perhaps I'd rob them
And tho I know you're dissatisfied with your position and your place
Don't you understand, it's not my problem?

I wish that for just one time you could stand inside my shoes
And just for that one moment I could be you
Yes, I wish that for just one time you could stand inside my shoes
You'd know what a drag it is to see you."

"Positively 4th Street" by Bob Dylan

"The Don"
29.07.2020

Bad Medicine

You are *"Witch's Brew"*.
You are *"snake's venom"*.
You are *"root of Hemlock"*.
You are *"poison ivy"*.
You are "Bad Blood".
You are *"rancid milk"*.
You are *"broken glass"*.
You are *"Bad News"*.
You are *"Rosemary's Baby"*.
You are *"Medusa"*.
You are *"Arachne"*.
You are *"Pandora with her box"*.
You are "*Salome with the head of John the Baptist*".
You are *"Cassandra"*.
You are *"Lilith"*.
You are *"Circe"*.
You are *"Medea"*.
You are *"Poison"*.
You are *"Evil"*.

You are a *"Voodoo Child"*.
You are a *"rattle snake"*.
You are a *"scorpion's tail"*.
You are a *"snake in the grass"*.
You are a *"spider's web"*.
You are a *"temptress"*.
You are a *"seducer"*.
You are a *"witch"*.
You are a *"sorceress"*.
You are a *"She-Devil"*.
You are a *"Siren"*.
You are a *"Gorgon"*.
You are a *"Hydra"*.
You are a *"Strega"*.
You are a *"Black Magic Woman"*.
You are a *"Devil Woman"*.
You are an *"enchantress"*.
You are an *"Evil Woman"*.

You have a *"fork tongue"*.
You have an *"Evil Eye"*.
You have the "Mark of Cain".
You have the *"Sign of the Devil"*.

You are the *"Black Widow"*.
You are the *"Devil's Child"*.

You are *"Bad Medicine"*.

"The Don"
31.07.2020

Let it Flow

Don't put barriers.
Don't put hurdles.
Don't put resistance.
Don't put pressure.
Don't put force.
Don't put obstacles in the way.
Just let it flow.

Allow things to evolve.
Allow things to take their own course.
Allow things to mature.
Allow things to have time.
Allow things to grow.
Allow things to ripen.
Allow things to energise.
Just let it flow.

Enjoy the process.
Enjoy the journey.
Enjoy the ride.
Enjoy the adventure.
Enjoy the sights.
Enjoy the view.
Enjoy the smells.
Enjoy the feelings.
Enjoy the fun.
Enjoy the Lo♥e.
Enjoy the people along the way.
Just let it flow.

Life's too short.
Life's too confusing.
Life's too complicated.
Life's too stressful.
Life's too complex.

Life's too meaningless.
Life's too problematic.
Life's too chaotic.
Life's too meaningless.
Just let it flow.

Just have fun.
Just Lo♥e everyone.
Just be a peace.
Just be free.
Just be.
Just let it flow.

Just open your eyes.
Just open your he♥rt.
Just open your soul.
Just open your mind.
Just let it flow.

Let it flow like a river.
Let it flow forever.
Let it flow eternally.
Let it flow to everyone.
Let it flow into the Cosmos.
Let it flow through you very "Being".
Let it flow to the very depths of your existence.
Let it flow without fear.
Let it flow without contradictions.
Let it flow without hesitations.
Let it flow without limits.
Let it flow like a torrent.
Let it flow for an eternity.
Let it flow beyond Death.
Let it flow through your Life.
Just let it flow.

"The Don"
31.07.2020

Que Sera Sera

(What Will Be, Will Be)

Will you be faithful?
Will you be true?
Will you Lo♥e me forever?
Will you promise me everlasting Lo♥e?
Will you always Lo♥e me?
Will you only Lo♥e me & no other!
Will you never Lo♥e another?
Will you be by my side forever?
Will you die by my side?
Will you always be enchanted by me?
Will you "bend the knee" to me?
Will you treat me like a princess?
Will you treat me like a queen?
Will you worship the very ground beneath my feet?
Will you actually kiss my feet!
Will you build a ladder to the stars?
Will you fly high?

*"Que sera sera
Whatever will be will be
The future's not ours to see
Que sera sera
What will be will be."*

*"When I was just a little girl
I asked my mother what will I be
Will I be pretty will I be rich?
Here's what she said to me*

*Que sera sera
Whatever will be will be
The future's not ours to see
Que sera sera
What will be will be*

When I grew up and fell in love
I asked my sweetheart what lies ahead
Will we have rainbows day after day
Here's what my sweetheart said

Que sera sera
Whatever will be will be
The future's not ours to see
Que sera sera
What will be will be

Now I have children of my own
They ask their mother what will I be
Will I be handsome will I be rich?
I tell them tenderly

Que sera sera
Whatever will be will be
The future's not ours to see
Que sera sera
What will be will be
Que sera sera."

Songwriters: Jay Livingston/Jean-christophe Le Saout/Galt Macdermot/Raymond B Evans

What Will Be, Will Be
(Que sera sera)

"The Don"
31.07.2020

Whatever Works for You

Do you have breakfast?
Do you have a large lunch?
Do you have a small dinner?
Do you snack in between?
Do you fast?
Do you "detox"?
Do you go on diets?
Do you eat meat?
Do you eat eggs?
Do you drink alcohol?
Do you smoke "dope"?
Do you fuck on the first date!

Do you believe in "True Lo♥e"?
Do you believe in "monogamy"?
Do you believe in "Polyamory"?
Do you believe in "Sin"?
Do you believe in "The Devil"?
Do you believe in "God", what "God" that is?

Do you trust politicians?
Do you trust the Government?
Do you trust "The System"?
Do you trust "The Establishment"?
Do you trust "The People"?
Do you trust your friends?
Do you trust yourself?

Do you believe in "Conspiracy Theories"?
Do you believe in "The Hidden Agenda"?
Do you believe in "State Terrorism"?
Do you believe in "Agenda 21"?
Do you believe in "The Club of Rome"?
Do you believe in "The Illuminati"?
Do you believe in "The Knights Templars"?
Do you believe in "Symbology"?
Do you believe in "Astrology"?
Do you believe in "Numerology"?
Do you believe in "The Paranormal"?
Do you believe in "The Spirit World"?

Do you believe in "Ghosts"?
Do you believe in "Spirituality"?
Do you believe in "Naturopathy"?
Do you believe in "Homeopathy"?
Do you believe in "Feng Shui"?
Do you believe in "Crystals"?
Do you believe in "Aromatherapy"?
Do you believe in "Karma"?
Do you believe in "Reincarnation"?
Do you believe in "Witchcraft"?
Do you believe in "Voodoo"?
Do you believe in "Superstition"?
Do you believe in "Out of Body Experiences"?
Do you believe in "Astral Travel"?
Do you believe in "Telekinesis"?
Do you believe in "Telepathy"?
Do you believe in "Life After Death"?
Do you believe in "Science"?
Do you believe in "Extraterrestrial Life"?
Do you believe in "Aliens"?
Do you believe in "Doomsday"?
Do you believe in "Humanity"?
Do you believe in "Yourself"?
Do you believe in "Me"?
Do you believe in "Bad"?
Do you believe in "Good"?
Do you believe in "LO♥E"?

Do you believe that Life is meaningless?
Do you believe that Life is a joke?
Do you believe that Life has a purpose?
Do you believe that Life has a meaning?

Just asking, "what works for you?"
Is okay by me.
Whatever it is you "believe in".
As long as it doesn't hurt others.
Is okay by me.
Whatever gets you through the night.
Whatever Works for You.
That's what I say!
Whatever Works for You!

"The Don"
01.08.2020

On the Edge of Forever

What will you *see*?
What will you *do*?
What will you *think*?
What will you *feel*?
What will you *hear*?
What will you *imagine*?
What will you *fear*?
What will you *dream*?
What will you *expect*?
What will you *want*?
What will you *hate*?
What will you *expect*?
What will you *desire*?
What will you *require*?
What will you *need*?
What will you *seed*?
What will you *eat*?
What will you *drink*?
What will you *fuck*?
What will you Lo ❤ e?

Will you be *scared*?
Will you be *afraid*?
Will you be *worried*?
Will you be *sad*?
Will you be *happy*?
Will you be *free*?
Will you be *adventurous*?
Will you be *timid*?
Will you be *courageous*?
Will you be *brave*?
Will you be *cowardly*?
Will you be *horrified*?
Will you be *petrified*?
Will you be *energised*?
Will you be *destroyed*?
Will you be *invigorated*?
Will you be *empowered*?
Will you be *enriched*?
Will you be *immortal*?
Will you be *Alive*?
Will you be *Dead*?
Will you be *"God"*?
Will you be "*The Devil*"?

What will you do, when you,
Stand on the *"Edge of Forever"*?

"The Don"
01.08.2020

What is Growing in Your Garden?

Are there flowers?
Sweet, perfumed roses, maybe?
Their fragrance so intoxicating.
Their beauty so exquisite.
Their colour so intense.

Are there *climing vines*?
Beautiful *"Boganvilias"*?
With their beautifully coloured flowers?
Reds, purples, pinks & blues.
But be careful!
Keep under them under control.
They grow very fast.
They will quickly get out of hand.
They will take over everything.
They have enormous branches.
There have enormous thorns.
Don't be deceived by their beauty.

The bright, sunny *"Sunflower"*.
The very exotic *"Waratah"*.
The alien-like *"Protea"*.
The romantic *"Cherry Blossom"*.
The exquisitely delicate *"Orchid"*.
The beautiful simplicity of the *"Tulip"*.
The amazingly beautiful *"Lily"*.

The extremely toxic *"Deadly Nightshade"*.
Which releases a poison that paralyses instantly!
"Water Hemlock", one of the world's most violently toxic plants.
The toxin acting directly on the central nervous system.
"Nerium Oleander", the sweetly scented killer.
"Castor oil plant", the most poisonous plant in the world.

What sorta garden are you growing?
Is a vegetable garden?
Is it a herb garden?
Is it an exotics garden?
Is it an indiginous garden?
Is it an ornamental garden?
Is it a manicured garden?
Is it a wild garden?

What sorta gardener are you?
Are you a careful gardener?
Are you a caring gardener?
Are you a Lo♥ing gardener?
Are you a "Bad" gardener?
Are you a "seeding" gardener?
Are you a nurturing gardener?
Are you a "watchful" gardener?

What sorta gardener are you?
One that makes sure the plants are happy?
One that waters them every day?
One that makes sure their soil is rich with nutrients?
One that talks to them & tells them how beautiful they are?
One that spends time with when they are sick & helps them get better?
One that feels them deeply, into his very soul?
One that cries when one dies, as if they were their child?

What sorta gardener are you?
What is growing in your garden?
Be careful what you grow in your garden?
Take care of your garden.
Make sure you are a good gardener.
This garden is inside of you.
Look after your *"Internal"* garden.
You take it with you wherever you go.
Give it a name.
Mine is called *"The Hanging Garden of Greek Street"*.
What is yours called?

𝔚𝔥𝔞𝔱 𝔦𝔰 𝔤𝔯𝔬𝔴𝔦𝔫𝔤 𝔦𝔫 𝔶𝔬𝔲𝔯 𝔤𝔞𝔯𝔡𝔢𝔫?

"Where have all the flowers gone, long time passing?
Where have all the flowers gone, long time ago?
Where have all the flowers gone?
Young girls have picked them, every one
Oh, when will they ever learn, oh when will they ever learn?

Where have all the husbands gone, long time passing?
Where have all the husbands gone, long time ago?
Where have all the husbands gone?
Gone for soldiers, every one
Oh, when will they ever learn, oh when will they ever learn?

Where have all the soldiers gone, long time passing?
Where have all the soldiers gone, long time ago?
Where have all the soldiers gone?
Gone to graveyards, every one
Oh, when will they ever learn, when will they ever learn?

Where have all the graveyards gone, long time passing?
Where have all the graveyards gone, long time ago?
Where have all the graveyards gone?
Gone to flowers, every one
Oh, when will they ever learn, oh when will they ever learn?"

Written by: Pete Seeger

"The Don"
03.08.2020

"It Depends on What Grows in Your Garden" (quilt)
By Mariclaire Pringle

I'm Stupid

I'm dumb.
I'm ignorant.
I know nothing at all.
I have no idea about anything.
I'm an imbicile.
I'm an idiot.
I'm crazy.
I'm mad.
I have no mind.
I am mind-less.
I have no brain.
I am brain-less.
I have no thought.
I am thought-less.

I have no idea what's going on.
I have no idea where I am.
I have no idea where I'm going.
I have no idea who I am.
I have no idea.
I am idea-less.

I am stoopid.
I am a "looney bin".
I know nothing.
"Stupidity" is my name.
I'm "that stoopid guy".
I'm stupid.

"The Don"
03.08.2020

I Will Not Let You Down

I've got your back.
I'll catch you if you fall.
I will always answer if you call.
I will always be there for you.

Don't panic.
Don't be scared.
Don't worry.
I'll be there.

Whenever you need me.
Whenever you're alone.
Whenever you want to share a moment.
I'll be there for you.

That is my promise.
That is my oath.
That is what I give to you.
My word, my truth.

I'll always be there.
No matter the reason.
I will not judge.
I am in no position to.

I am your friend.
This is what I am.
This what I do.
This is the only thing I can do.

I will not let you down.

"The Don"
03.08.2020

The Garden of Earthly Delights

(Il Giardino delle Delizie Terrene)

What do Desire?
What do you want?
What do require?
What do you need?

It's all here.
Whatever your heart desires.
Sex, drugs, rock & roll?
It's all here & much more.

There are girls galore.
There are boys & more.
There is S & M.
There is bondage.

There are no morals here.
Anything & everything goes.
There are no taboos.
There are no boundaries.
There are NO rules.
This is the place where your dreams are fulfilled!

You can have as much pussy as you can handle.
You can have as much cock as you mouth can take.
You can drink as much as you can swallow.
You can smoke as much dope as you can inhale.

You can eat as much food as you can swallow.
You can inject as much heroin as the number of veins in your body.
You can fuck as long as your cock can stay hard.
You can suck as long as your tongue can take.
You can lick until your mouth has become dry.
You can kiss until your lips become numb.
You can feel finger until you have a cramp.

You can enjoy yourself until your time has run out.
You can stay as long as you like.
You can stay until you've satisfied your insatiable appetite.
You can stay forever if that's what you want.
You can die here if that's how you want to end your days.

"The Don"
03.08.2020

Ownership

(Possession)

You must understand this.
This must be very clear.
Let's make no mistake about this.
There is no ambiguity.
You cannot own a person.

You cannot own another person.
You cannot possess another Human Being.
No matter what you have told.
No matter what you may think.
You can own another person.

You cannot own another person's Lo♥e.
You cannot own another person's Lo♥e exclusively.
You cannot stop a person from Lo♥ing others.
You cannot own Lo♥e.

A person is not an object you can own.
A person is not an object you can possess.
A person cannot be kept a prisoner by another.
A person cannot be told that they cannot any other.
A person cannot be told that you are the only person they can Lo♥e.
A person cannot be told that you are the only person that they must Lo♥e.
A person cannot be told that you are the only person that they must Lo♥e, FOREVER.

A person should not be made to feel guilty for Lo♥ing others.
A person should not be made to feel bad for Lo♥ing others.
A person should not be made to suffer for Lo♥ing others.
A person should not be made to feel inhuman for Lo♥ing others.

A person should not be made to feel free to Lo♥ing others.
A person should not be made to feel happy for Lo♥ing others.
A person should not be made to feel ecstatic for Lo♥ing others.
A person should not be made to feel human for Lo♥ing others.

Lo♥ing someone does not mean that you own them.
Ownership has nothing to do with Lo♥e.
Understand this simple fact & set them free.
Then & only then will the possibility of "True Lo♥e" arise.
"If you Lo♥e somebody, set them free!
Free, free, set them free!"

"The Don"
04.08.2020

Brain-Dead
(Morte Cerebrale)

Don't see!
Don't observe!
Don't read!
Don't write!
Don't discuss!
Don't converse!
Don't exchange!
Don't interact!
Don't communicate!
Don't theorise!
Don't hypothesise!

Don't feel!
Don't act!
Don't react!
Don't move!
Don't object!
Don't reject!
Don't protest!
Don't disagree!
Don't contradict!
Don't rebel!
Don't Lo♥e!
Don't THINK!

You are "Brain-Dead"!

"The Don"
05.08.2020

Objectification
(Dehumanisation)

I am not an object!
I am not a thing!
I am not a piece of merchandise.
I am not a piece of jewellery.
I am not your personal toy.
I am not your personal plaything.
I am not a piece of meat.
I am not a lump of lard.
I am not a stupid thing.
I am not a baby.
I am not a sex doll.
I am not a slave.
I am not a fool.
I am not a tool.
I am not a trophy.
I am not a handbag.
I am not a piece of rag.
I am not a piece of "merda".
I am not a "slut".
I am not a "whore".
I am not a "cunt".
I am not a "cunt face".
I am not a "shit face".
I am not a "troll".

I am much, much more.
I am a *Human Being*!

So, treat me with *RESPECT*!

"The Don"
05.08.2020

𝕴 𝖆𝖒 𝖆𝖓 𝕴𝖓𝖉𝖎𝖛𝖎𝖉𝖚𝖆𝖑

(Sono un Individuo)

I do not belong to anyone.
I am not a possession.
I cannot be bought & sold.
I am not an object.
I am not something to be *"used & abused"*.
I am not a *"plaything"*.
I am not here to satisfy your *"personal appetites"*.
I am not your *"object of desire"*.
I am not your slave.
I am not your toy.
I am not your possession.
I am not yours.

I am an independent person.
I am *"my own"* person.
I am independent.
I am self-reliant
I am intelligent.
I am smart.
I am passionate.
I am resilient.
I am strong.
I am independent.
I am powerful.
I am creative.
I am Human.

I have my own mind.
I have my own feelings.
I have my own thoughts.
I have my own ideas.
I have my own hands
I have my own legs.
I have my own head.
I have my own body.
I have my own Will.
I have my own Mind.
I have my own He❤rt.

I do not have a price!

I am a Human Being.

I am an Individual.

"The Don"
05.08.2020

The Devil's Hand
(La Mano del Diavolo)

Things not working out?
Chaos about?
World gone crazy?
Everyone's lazy?
Sinners abound?
Madness going round?
The end of the World is here?
Armageddon is near?
Destruction about?
People not let out?
Fever in the air?
It's contagious, I swear?
Are you alright?

No Lo♥e at first sight?
Fish are dying in the river?
You don't like chicken liver?
Your hands are as cold as ice.
You've paid a very high price.
Don't stick your head in the sand.
It's the Devil's Hand.

"The Don"
06.08.2020

Love is......
(L'amore è......)

Love is tough.
Love is strong.
Love is flexible.
Love is maleable.
Love is ductile.
Love is adaptable.
Love is flexible.
Love is expandable!
Love is elastic.
Love is limitless.
Love is infinite.
Love is inexhaustible.
Love is unbreakable.
Love is renewable.
Love is rejuvenating.
Love is unending.
Love is bottomless.

"The Don"
06.08.2020

Don't Be So Precious

(Non Essere Così Prezioso)

Don't be so precious with your *Lo♥e*.
Don't be so precious with your *body*.
Don't be so precious with your *mind*.
Don't be so precious with your *thoughts*.
Don't be so precious with your *feelings*.
Don't be so precious with your *He♥rt*.
Don't be so precious with your *soul*.
Don't be so precious with your *ideas*.
Don't be so precious with your *humour*.
Don't be so precious with your *laughter*.
Don't be so precious with your *smile*.
Don't be so precious with your *hugs*.
Don't be so precious with your *kisses*.
Don't be so precious with your *fucking*.
Don't be so precious with your *warmth*.
Don't be so precious with your *bed*.
Don't be so precious with your *food*.
Don't be so precious with your *meals*.
Don't be so precious with your *table*.
Don't be so precious with your *shower*.
Don't be so precious with your *bath*.
Don't be so precious with your *home*.
Don't be so precious with your *money*.
Don't be so precious with your *time*.
Don't be so precious with your *eyes*.
Don't be so precious with your *songs*.

Don't be so precious with whom you *sleep*.
Don't be so precious with whom you *sing*.
Don't be so precious with whom you *laugh*.
Don't be so precious with whom you *fuck*.
Don't be so precious with whom you share your *body with*.
Don't be so precious with whom you share your *Lo♥e*.
Don't be so precious with whom you *Lo♥e*.

"The Don"
06.08.2020

Imagine

Imagine Creativity.
Imagine Beauty.
Imagine Harmony.
Imagine Freedom.
Imagine Democracy.
Imagine Humanity.
Imagine Liberty.
Imagine Justice.
Imagine Spirituality.
Imagine Reality.
Imagine Respect.
Imagine Compassion.
Imagine Friendship.
Imagine Equality.
Imagine Fairness.
Imagine Satisfaction.
Imagine Truth.
Imagine Forever.
Imagine Infinity.
Imagine Subjectivity.
Imagine Non-existence.
Imagine Death.
Imagine Life.
Imagine Sensuality.
Imagine Seeing.
Imagine Feeling.
Imagine Being.
Imagine Soulfulness.
Imagine Wonderness.
Imagine Transcendence.
Imagine Mindfulness.
Imagine Happiness.
Imagine Lo♥e.
Imagine Imagination!
"I wonder if you can?"

"The Don"
07.08.2020

Terrific

Spectacularific
Surrealific
Cosmific.
Atmospherific.
Humanific.
Orgasmicific.
Coolerrific.
Fuckerrific.
Beautific.
Peacific.
Fabulerrific.
Fantasterrific.
Awesomerific.
Futurific.
Spaceific.
Artisterrific.
Createrrific.
Creatific.
Weirdific.
Crazific.
Mindific.
Mindlessific.
Brainific.
Brainlessific.
Braindeadific.
Donific.
Wonderific.
Lo♡ific.

"The Don"
07.08.2020

Treaty

Treaty for *recognition* of who you are.
Treaty for *stealing* your land.
Treaty for past *sins*.
Treaty for *raping* the women.
Treaty for the *"Stolen General"*.
Treaty for destroying *"Sacred sites"*.
Treaty for having had no *"Rights"*.
Treaty for *Respect*.
Treaty for being *"First Nation's Peoples"*.
Treaty for being the *"Oldest Surviving Culture"* in the World today.
Treaty for all the *wrongs* that were made.
Treaty for *equality*.
Treaty for the *Future*.

Treaty to enshrine your *"Rights"*.
Treaty to admit the *wrongs made*.
Treaty to make it *"Right"*.
Treaty to make *amends*.
Treaty to say, *"SORRY"*.
Treaty to make it *"Law"*.
Treaty to be written in *"The Constitution"*.
Treaty to make a *"New Start"*.
Treaty to stop the "Fight".
Treaty to recognise that *"Black Lives Matter"*.

*"Well I heard it on the radio
And I saw it on the television
Back in 1988
All those talking politicians
Words are easy, words are cheap
Much cheaper than our priceless land
But promises can disappear
Just like writing in the sand*

*Treaty Yeh Treaty Now
Treaty Yeh Treaty Now*

*Nhima Djatpangarri nhima walangwalang -
Nhe Djatpayatpa nhima gaya nhe-
Matjini.... Yakarray - nhe Djat'pa nhe walang - Gumurrtijararrk Gutjuk —"*

"This land was never given up
This land was never bought and sold
The planting of the Union Jack
Never changed our law at all

Now two rivers run their course
Separated for so long
I'm dreaming of a brighter day
When the waters will be one

Treaty Yeh Treaty Now Treaty Yeh Treaty Now
Treaty Yeh Treaty Now Treaty Yeh Treaty Now

Nhima djatpa nhe walang
gumurrtjararrk yawirriny Nhe gaya nhe matjini
Gaya nhe matjini Gaya gaya nhe gaya nhe
Matjini walangwalang Nhema djatpa nhe walang - Nhe gumurrtjarrk nhe ya-

Promises - Disappear - Priceless land - Destiny -

Well I heard it on the Radio - And I saw it on the Television
But promises can be broken Just like writing in the sand

Treaty Yeh
Treaty Now ...."

Songwriters: Stuart Adam Kellaway/Paul Maurice Kelly/Witiyana Philip Marika/Milkayngu Mununggurr/Cal Stanley Williams/Gurrumul Yunupingu/Mandawuy Bakamana Yunupingu

Treaty NOW!

"The Don"
08.08.2020

"Because of Her We can!"
By Kathryn Dodd Farrawell

Relationships

Relationships *suffocate* me.
Relationships don't allow me to *breathe*.
Relationships put *words* into my mouth.

Relationships want to *control* me.
Relationships want to *tell* me what to *do*.
Relationships want to *define* me.
Relationships want to *own* me.
Relationships want to *imprison* me.
Relationships want to *restrict* me.

Relationships think they know who I *am*.
Relationships think they know how I *feel*.
Relationships think they *understand* me.
Relationships think they *know* me.
Relationships deny my *Freedom*.

Relationships can *scare* me.
Relationships can *disturb* me.
Relationships can *overpower* me.
Relationships can *devour* me.

Relationships can be *dangerous*.
Relationships can be *violent*.
Relationships can be *abusive*.
Relationships can be about *"Control"*.
Relationships can be about *"Power"*.
Relationships can be about *"Possession"*.
Relationships can be FUCKED.

Relationships are *complicated*.
Relationships are *complex*.
Relationships are *important*.
Relationships are *necessary*.
Relationships are *"Everything"*.
Relationships are not about Lo♥e.

Relationships should be about Lo♥e.
Relationships should be *beautiful*.
Relationships should be *liberating*.
Relationships should be *invigorating*.
Relationships should be *rewarding*.
Relationships should be *"fluidic"*.
Relationships should be *"evolving"*.
Relationships should be *"growing"*.
Relationships should be about *"letting go"*.

Relationships are about *"Oneself"*.
Relationships are about *"who you are"*.
Relationships are in your *"Mind"*.
Relationships are defined by the type of relationship you have with *"Yourself"*.
Relationships are about *"Me"*!

"The Don"
08.08.2020

Live in the Moment

(Vivi nel Momento)

Be spontaneous.
Be instantaneous.
Be unplanned.
Be uncontrolled.
Be unstructured.
Be instantaneous.
Be flexible.
Be "Fluidic".
Be unpredictable.
Be adventurous.
Be risky.
Be "Open".
Be frivolous.
Be fun.
Be humourous.
Be funny.
Be unpredictable.
Be momentary.
Be "Open".
Be "available".
Be adaptable.
Be "COOL".
Be "Undefinable".
Be "Uncontrollable".
Be Lo♥eable.

Live in the Moment!

"The Don"
08.08.2020

Things People Say That Irritate Me
(Cose che le Persone Dicono che mi Irritano)

"You're a *player*"
"You're back in the *game*"
"You can *settle down*"
"You've *settled down*"
"You should *settle down*"
"*Grow* up"
"**Act** your age"
"*Slow down*"
"Where's your *woman*?"
"Where's your *man*?"
"Where's your "*other*" half?"
"Where's your "*better*" half?"
"You *talk* too much"
"You *can't say* that"
"Don't *swear*"
"You *swear* too much"
"Don't say "Lo♥e you!" to complete strangers"
"You put people *off*"
"You're *offensive*"
"It's *too early* in the morning to say that"
"You're too *loud*"
"You've *overstepped* the line"
"You can only Lo♥e one person"
"You're being *unfaithful*"
"But, you're in a *relationship*!"
"You can only be in *one* relationship at a time!"
"You *have* (enter name of person here)"
"Are you a *couple*?"
"Are you in a *relationship*?"
"You're not in a *relationship*?"
"Are you *seeing* anyone?"
"Are you seeing anyone *special*?"
"Is there anyone special in *your life*?"
"Do you have a *partner*?"
"Is that your *floozy*?"
"You've got *someone*"
"You don't get *lonely*?"
"You're too *old*!"

"The Don"
09.08.2020

Dog My Cat

Cat my dog.
Baby, baby, you know where it's at.
Fish my beaver.
Squirrel my bird.
Worm my cow.
Tiger my giraffe.
Meerkat my lion.
Crocodile my emu.
Buffalo my gazelle.
Donkey my hyena.
Gorilla my snake.
Lorikeet my ferret.
Gerbil my platypus.
Ostrich my bat.
Koala Bear my Gangaroo (kangaroo).
Deer my wolf.
Fox my penguin.
Rhinoceros my turkey.
Goat my panda.
Leopard my monkey.
Squirrel my otter.
Hippopotamus my chicken.
Parrot my shark.
Butterfly my raccoon.
Goanna my hedgehog.
Weasel my duck.
Rabbit my wombat.
Echidna my sloth.
Ant my camel.
Lemur my moose.
Human my ape.

"The Don"
09.08.2020.

I Lo♥e You

(but I'm Not "In Lo♥e" with You)

There seems to be a confusion here.
There seems to be a misunderstanding.
There seems to be an error in communication.
There seems to be complication.
There seems to be misinterpretation.
There seems to be a miscommunication.
"I Lo♥e" you (but I'm not *"in Lo♥e"* with you).

What is this confusion?
What is this misunderstanding?
What is this error in communication?
What is this complication?
What is this misinterpretation?
What is this miscommunication?
"I Lo♥e" you (but I'm not *"in Lo♥e"* with you).

So, let's put right.
Let's put straight!
Let's rectify this confusion.
Let's correct this misunderstanding.
Let's sort out this error in communication.
Let's simplify this complication.
Let's fix this misinterpretation.
Let's solve this miscommunication.
"I Lo♥e" you (but I'm not *"in Lo♥e"* with you).

"I Lo♥e" is *friendship*.
"I Lo♥e" is *companionship*.
"I Lo♥e" is *respect*.
"I Lo♥e" is *caring*.
"I Lo♥e" is *kindness*.
"I Lo♥e" is *compassion*.
"I Lo♥e" is *sharing*.
"I Lo♥e" is *teamwork*.
"I Lo♥e" is *mutual agreement*.
"I Lo♥e" is *understanding*.
"I Lo♥e" is <u>*domestic arrangements*</u>.
"I Lo♥e" is *fucking*.
"I Lo♥e" is *sex*.
"I Lo♥e" is *Lo♥e*.
"I Lo♥e" you (but I'm not *"in Lo♥e"* with you).

"I Lo♥e" can become *commitment*.
"I Lo♥e" can become *obligation*.
"I Lo♥e" can become *obligatory*.
"I Lo♥e" can become *ritualised*.
"I Lo♥e" can become *stylised*.
"I Lo♥e" can become *compromised*.
"I Lo♥e" can become *compartmentalised*.
"I Lo♥e" can become *sterilised*.
"I Lo♥e" can become *marginalised*.
"I Lo♥e" can become *formulised*.
"I Lo♥e" can become *formulaic*.
"I Lo♥e" can become *routine*.
"I Lo♥e" can become *boring*.
"I Lo♥e" can become *familiarity*.
"I Lo♥e" can become *regularity*.
"I Lo♥e" can become *regulated*.
"I Lo♥e" can become *conceited*.
"I Lo♥e" can become *simplistic*.
"I Lo♥e" can become *fragile*.
"I Lo♥e" can become *stale*.
"I Lo♥e" can become *unimaginative*.
"I Lo♥e" can become *repetitive*.
"I Lo♥e" can become *stale*.
"I Lo♥e" can become *smelly*.
"I Lo♥e" can become *disastrous*.
"I Lo♥e" can become *abuse*.
"I Lo♥e" can become *imprisonment*.
"I Lo♥e" can become *enchainment*.
"I Lo♥e" can become *confinement*.
"I Lo♥e" can become *possession*.
"I Lo♥e" can become *possessive*.
"I Lo♥e" can become *objectified*.
"I Lo♥e" can become *destructive*.
"I Lo♥e" can become *harassment*.
"I Lo♥e" can become *soul-destroying*.
"I Lo♥e" can become *hatred*.
"I Lo♥e" can become "I HATE".
"I Lo♥e" can become VIOLENCE.
"I Lo♥e" can become a NIGHTMARE.
"I Lo♥e" can become DEATH.
"I Lo♥e" can become HELL.
"I Lo♥e" you (but I'm not "*in Lo♥e*" with you).

"In Lo♥e" is Passion.
"In Lo♥e" is Desire.
"In Lo♥e" is Fire.
"In Lo♥e" is Orgasmic.
"In Lo♥e" is "Making Lo♥e".
"In Lo♥e" is emersion.
"In Lo♥e" is submersion.
"In Lo♥e" is Oneness.
"In Lo♥e" is Ecstasy.
"In Lo♥e" is Heavenly.
"In Lo♥e" is Euphoria.
"In Lo♥e" is Euphoric.
"In Lo♥e" is Spectacularific.
"In Lo♥e" is Intimicy.
"In Lo♥e" is Sensuality.
"In Lo♥e" is Sexuality.
"In Lo♥e" is Erotic.
"In Lo♥e" is Eroticism.
"In Lo♥e" is Sublimific.
"In Lo♥e" is instantaneous.
"In Lo♥e" is emersion.
"In Lo♥e" is "Losing oneself".
"In Lo♥e" is fleeting.
"In Lo♥e" is emersion.
"I Lo♥e" you (but I'm not "in Lo♥e" with you).

"I Lo♥e" you
(but I'm not "in Lo♥e" with you)

"The Don"
10.08.2020

It ALL Works Out in the End!

(Alla Fine Funziona Tutto!)

Don't stress.
Don't panic.
Don't fret.
Don't fear.
Don't manipulate.
Don't control.
Don't lose it.
Don't push it.
Don't force it.
Don't have expectations.
It ALL works out in the end!

Don't get angry.
Don't get sad.
Don't get depressed.
Don't get disappointed.
It ALL works out in the end!

Don't moan.
Don't bitch.
Don't whinge.
Don't shout.
Don't scream.
Don't cry.
Don't get disheartened.
Don't get disillusioned.
Don't get violent.
It ALL works out in the end!

Let it flow.
Let it happen.
Let it take its own course.
Let it evolve.
Let it reach a conclusion.
Let it reach the End.
It ALL works out in the end!

Everything sorts itself out.
Everything has a solution.
Everything has an answer.
Everything is an adventure.
Everything is a ride.
Everything is a journey.
Everything is an experience.
Everything works out.
Everything works out in the End!

It ALWAYS does.
If it hasn't, it's not the End, yet!
It ALWAYS works out in the end!

Just accept this fundamental fact.
It ALL works out in the end!

It ALL Works Out in the End!

"The Don"
11.08.2020

The Demon Hunter

"Come out, come out!
Demons are about!"

Demons are hiding.
Demons are lurking.
Demons are everywhere.
Demons are in the attic.
Demons are in the cellar.
Demons are in the kitchen.
Demons are in the bedroom.
Demons are in your bed.
Demons are under your bed.
Demons are flying around you.
Hell, Demons are in your HEAD.

Watch out, watch out!
Demons are about.
They are everywhere.

You can't run.
You can't hide.
You can't escape.
You can't move.
You can't cry.
You can't shout.
You can't scream.
You can't flee.
You can't see.
You can't hear
You can't think.

Watch out, watch out!
Demons are about.

They want to do you harm.
They want to eat you alive.
They want to see you scream.
They want to terrorise you.
They want to give you nightmares.
They want to give you night sweats.
They want to make you scared.
They want to terrorise you.
They want to get inside you HEAD.
They want to control you.
Hell, they want to see you DEAD.

Watch out, watch out!
Demons are about.
They are everywhere.

You've gotta be strong.
You've gotta be brave.
You've gotta be fearless.
You've gotta be powerful.
You've gotta be smart.
You've gotta be thinking.
You've gotta be resolute.
You've gotta be firm.

Watch out, watch out!
Demons are about.

You've gotta stand your ground.
You've gotta have your wits about you.
You've gotta not you let you guard down.
You've gotta choose the right time.
You've gotta choose the right place.
You've gotta choose the right moment.
You've gotta be well prepared.

Watch out, watch out!
Demons are about.

You've gotta act fast.
You've gotta act swiftly.
You've gotta act precisely.
You've gotta act cleanly.
You've gotta act clearly.
You've gotta act fearlessly.
You've gotta act DEMONIC.

Watch out, watch out!
Demons are about.

"Come out, come out!
Demons are about!
You can't hide from me.

I'm the DEMON HUNTER!"

"The Don"
12.08.2020

We All Wear a Mask

(Tutti Indossiamo una Maschera)

Who are you?
Who are you really?

Who are you pretending to be?
Who would you like to be?
Who do you think you are?
Who is the "REAL" you?
Who is the "FAKE" you?

Who are you?
Who are you really?

Who are you in your head?
Who are you in your thoughts?
Who are you in your dreams?
Who are you in your nightmares?
Who are you with your family?
Who are you with your friends?
Who are you with your Lo♥er?
Who are you when you're walking down the street?
Who are you with complete strangers?
Who are you when you are at work?
Who are you when you are happy?
Who are you when you are upset?
Who are you when you are sad?
Who are you when you are angry?
Who are you when you fuck?
Who are you when you make Lo♥e?

Who are you?
Who are you really?

Who is that person looking through your eyes?
Who is the person behind your mask?
Who are you when you take off your mask?

Who are you?
Who are you really?

"The Don"
13.08.2020

You Choose Your Own Emotions

(Tu Scegliere le tue Emozioni)

What do you choose?
What Do you want to be?

Do you want to be *happy*?
Do you want to be *high*?
Do you want to be *ecstatic*?
Do you want to be *euphoric*?
Do you want to be *Lo♥ing*?
Do you want to be *passionate*?
Do you want to be *stressed*?
Do you want to be *dramatic*?
Do you want to be *sad*?
Do you want to be *depressed*?
Do you want to be *angry*?
Do you want to be *violent*?
Do you want to be *aggressive*?
Do you want to be *abusive*?
DO you want to be *hateful*?
Do you want to be *brutal*?
Do you want to be *mad*?
Do you want to be *crazy*?
Do you want to be *uncontrollable*?
Do you want to be *indulgent*?
Do you want to be *jealous*?
Do you want to be *pathetic*?
Do you want to be *miserable*?
Do you want to be *heartfelt*?
Do you want to be *sincere*?
Do you want to be *trusting*?
Do you want to be *friendly*?
Do you want to be *kind*?
Do you want to be *concerned*?
Do you want to be *unconcerned*?
Do you want to be *genuine*?
Do you want to be *unconventional*?
Do you want to be *free*?
Do you want to be *dreamy*?
Do you want to be *sexy*?
Do you want to be *sensual*?
Do you want to be *emotional*?
Do you want to be *unemotional*?

YOU choose your own emotions.

"The Don"
13.08.2020

The triumph of IDIOCY & STUPIDITY!

These are strange days that we are living in.
These are strange times that we are living in.
These are strange days indeed!

These are strange people who are in governments.
They are strange people who are in power.
These are strange people who are making decisions.
These are strange people that are making the rules.
These are strange people that are ruling our minds.
These are strange people that are ruining our lives.
These are strange people that are that are destroying the world.
These are strange people that are destroying the planet.

These are strange people that don't know what they are doing.
These are strange people that don't know what they are saying.
These are strange people that don't know anything at all.
These are strange people that don't know a FUCKING thing!

These are strange day where idiocy & stupidity rule.
These are strange day where ignorance is rewarded.
These are strange day where stupidity is applauded.
These are strange day where lunatics have taken over the asylum.
These are strange day where idiots are in control.
These are strange day where stupidity is at the helm.

These are the days where idiocy has triumphed.
These are the days where stupidity is triumphant.
These are the days where lunatics have won.
These are the days where intelligence has died.
These are the days where science is DEAD.
These are the days where we must all run & hide.

These are the days when "The Light" has been put out.
These are the days when "The Darkness" has descended.
These are the days when FEAR is in control.
These are the days when "The End" is near.
These are the days when we all say our prays.
These are the days when DEATH is here.

For these are the days of the "Triumph of IDIOCY & STUPIDITY"!

"The Don"
13.08.2020

The Best Laid Plans Of Mice & Men

(I Migliori Piani di Topi e Uomini)

They're bound to *fail*.
They can't *succeed*.
You'll be *disappointed*.

You're heading for a *fall*.
You're gonna be *sad*.
You're gonna be *hurt*.
You're too *connected*.
You're emotionally *invested*.
You're not *disconnected*.
You're letting your imagination run away with you.

You want it too badly.
You can't stop thinking about it.

It's inside your *brain*.
It's inside your *head*.
It's inside your He♥rt.
It's inside your *gut*.
It's inside your *blood*.
It's under your *skin*.
It's making you feel *dead*.

You have to *disconnect*.
You have to *step back*.
You have to *regain control*.
You have to *let it go*.
You have to *breathe deeply*.
You have to *count to ten*.
You have to *accept failure*.

You can't let this happen again.
You've been here before.
You know what's the score.
You know how this will end.
You know the *"End game"*.
You know what the outcome will be.
You can predict the Future.
You see it all coming.

Are you going to something about it?
Before it's too late.
It's already here.
It's knocking on your gate.
It's at the front door.
Are you gonna let it in!
Are you gonna let it all fall?
Those best laid plans of mice & men!

For, "The best laid plans of mice & men often go awry"!

The Best Laid Plans Of Mice & Men

"The Don"
14.08.2020

False Gods

(Falsi Dei)

Whom do you worship?
To whom do you pray?
Whom do you idolise?
With whom do you lay?

Do you worship the God of money?
Who will buy you everything you ever want!
Do you worship material objects?
In the hope that they will fill the emptiness you have inside.
Do you surround with things of every description?
Do you live in a mansion?
Do you hear the echo of your own footsteps?
In the empty halls of your castle?
The emptiness of your prison?
For you have no friends!

Do you worship the God of Prestige?
Do you worship at its altar?
Do you kiss & lick its feet?
Do you pray for fame & glory?
Maybe, to be a movie star?
Like Marilyn Monroe or George Clooney?
Celluloid Heroes that will never really die.
Do you want to be idolised?
Do you want to be revered?
Do you want to be remembered?
Even after you are Dead?

Do you worship the God of Power?
Do you seek to want to rule?
To be a monarch or a world leader?
Maybe, the President of The United States of America?
Do you want to have total control?
To make people do whatever you want?
Do you see yourself like Julius Caesar or maybe, Donald Trump?
Do you want to rule the World?
Have people kiss your hand & lick your arse.

Do you want to be all powerful?
You have statues erected to yourself.
You face is everywhere, on the walls & on the streets.
Flags have you face painted on them.
Shit, your face is even on the dollar bill.
You have monuments dedicated to your greatness.
You are idolised & worshipped as a God.
Fuck, what am I saying, you are a fucking God!
At least in your tiny, idiotic, stupid HEAD!

Do you worship the God of Pleasure?
Do you pray at its sumptuous altar?
Do you seek pleasure in all its forms?
Do you want to fulfill you every insatiable desire?
Do you want to try the forbidden fruits?
Be intoxicated by its perfume?
Get drunk on its alcohol?
Get feed on its exotic foods?
Do you wanna sit at the beggar's banquet?
Do you wanna watch Salome do her dance?
Do want to feed on the head of John the Baptist?
As it is passed around on it tray?

Do want to sip from "Golden Chalice"?
The one that was used on that treacherous night,
By Jesus at "the last supper"?
Do you want to set your eyes upon "The Holy Grail"?
To gain its powers & it's might.
Do you want to experience every carnal delight?
Do you want to wallow in all "Earthly Pleasures"?
Do want to be swallowed by the serpent of the flesh.

Do want to remain forever in the "House of Human Pleasures"?
To lock the door & live forever?
A prisoner in the "House of Sin"!

(False Gods)

"The Don"
14.08.2020

The Human Academy
(L'Accademia Umana)

It teaches you how to be Humane.
It teaches you how to be Humble.
It teaches you how to be Kind.
It teaches you how to be Caring.
It teaches you how to be Respectful.
It teaches you how to be Compassionate.
It teaches you how to be Friendly.
It teaches you how to be Co-operative.
It teaches you how to be Intelligent.
It teaches you how to be Creative.
It teaches you how to be Lo♥ing.
It teaches you how to be Soulful.
It teaches you how to be Non-Violent.
It teaches you how to be Silent.
It teaches you how to be HUMAN.

It will teach you about Enlightenment.
It will teach you about Spirituality.
It will teach you about "The Look Within".
It will teach you about "The Internal Landscape".
It will teach you about "Human Landscape".
It will teach you about "Self-knowledge".
It will teach you about "The Force".
It will teach you about "The Light".
It will teach you about "The Consciousness".
It will teach you about "The Journey".
It will teach you about "How to begin".
It will teach you about "Transcendence".
It will teach you about "Transference".
It will teach you about "Meditation".
It will teach you about "Death".

It will show you "Ancient Knowledge".
Long ago forgotten.
It will show you how to live your life,
Without "Pain & Suffering".
It will show you pathways to the "Healing of Suffering".
It will show you the path to "Inner Peace".
The one we all struggle for but never, ever achieve.
The "Knowledge" not given to us, by our "Social Academy".

So, if you're interested in such things.
If you are curious about such matters.
If I've piqued your curiosity.
Seek us out.
You'll find us.
We're not that hard to find.
Just follow the signs.
They are everywhere.
You just have to open your eyes.
As if you are looking through them,
For the very first time!

The Human Academy

"The Don"
14.08.2020

Personas

Being yourself is boring.
Who do you want to be?
Who are you now?
At this very precise moment!

Are you *Marilyn Monroe*?
Are you *Greta Garbo*?
Are you *Fay Dunaway*?
Are you *Madonna*?
Are you *Patti Smith*?
Are you *Hayley Quinn*?
Are you *Kim Kardashian*?
Are you *Ruby Rose*?
Are you *Cleopatra*?
Are you *Queen Nefertiti*?
Are you *Beyonce*?

You can't be "yourself".
Being "yourself" is very boring.
In fact, you don't even know who you are.
And whomever you think you are,
You're not very good at.

You have issues with *self-image*.
You have issues with *self-worth*.
You have issues with *self-doubt*.
You have issues with *self-belief*.
You have issues with *loneliness*.
You have issues with *rejection*.
You have issues with *abandonment*.
You have issues with *failure*.
You have issues with *Death*.

You think you are not *very pretty*.
You think you are *too ugly*.
You think you are *too fat*.
You think you are *too tall*.
You think you are *too short*.
You think you are *not smart enough*.
You think you are *not good enough*.

You just can't be yourself.
You gotta be someone else.

Someone who *is perfect*.
Someone who *can do no wrong*.
Someone who *is a "superhero"*.
Someone who is a "*success story*".
Someone who is *smart*.
Someone who is *rich*.
Someone who is *famous*.
Someone who is *great*.
Someone who all these things & more.

Choose your persona.
Mix & match if you have the mind to.
There is nothing to say "you can't".
There is no rule book.
In fact, there are no rules.
Be whomever you want to be.
Don't let anyone or anything stand in your way.

Although this is a "Cautionary Tale".
There is a sting in the scorpion's tail.
"Don't identity too closely, with this imaginary you.
Don't lose yourself to it.
Because if you do, you may get trapped.
And may never be able to get out!"

This is the "fine line" that you must walk.
To make sure you can find you way back.
You must leave some crumbs,
So, that you have a pathway you can follow.
Back to yourself.
Otherwise, you'll be lost forever as your persona.
Never being able to come back.

"The Don"
15.08.2020

Guys Just Want to Fuck

(I Ragazzi Vogliono Solo Scopare)

See a girl.
See a chick.
See a babe.
See a Hot babe.

First thought in my mind.
First thing I want to do.
I want to fuck you.
I didn't care where.
Just then & there will do.
I actually, haven't really thought it through.
But the only thing I know.
Is, *I just want to fuck you*.

By "you", I mean anyone will do.
Nothing personal.
It's just I do.
It's just how I think.
It's just how I'm wired.
It must be in my DNA or something?
I don't really know.
I haven't really given it too much thought.
To be honest with you.
It's just what I do.
I just want to fuck you.

You can be tall or short.
Not too fat.
Not too skinny.
But you must have boobies & a booty.
These are essentials.
You must be "sexy".
Which is so hard to define.
It's whatever turns me on
You also have "attitude".
My cock will decide.
It will tell me straight away
I just want to fuck you.
And there's nothing more to say.

"The Don"
15.08.2020

Toy Boy

I'll be your handbag.
I'll be your glad bag.
I'll be your paper bag.
I'll be your plastic bag.
I'll be your carry bag.
I'll be your library bag.
I'll be your shopping bag.
I'll be your day bag.
I'll be your night bag.
I'll be your take away bag.
I'll be your overnight bag.
I'll be your travel bag.
I'll be your rubbish bag.
I'll be your used bag.
I'll be your abused bag.
I'll be your douche bag.
I'll be your reusable bag.
I'll be your recycled bag.
I'll be your green bag.
I'll be your cosmetic bag.
I'll be your beauty bag.
I'll be your personal bag.
I'll be your accessories bag.
I'll be your necessities bag.
I'll be your clothes bag.
I'll be your laundry bag
I'll be your toy bag.
I'll be your man bag.
I'll be your anything bag.
I'll be your Lo♥e bag.

"The Don"
16.08.2020

Ego IS a Dirty Word

(L'ego è una Parolaccia)

If I did not have an ego I would still be here tonight.
If I did not have an ego, I would still think that I was right.
If you did not have an ego you would still care about the way you dressed.
If you did not have an ego, you'd be better than the rest!

Ego is IS a dirty word.
You should believe what you've seen & heard.

If Kurt Cobain had no ego, he'd still be alive today.
And if Trump had no ego, he would still be in decay.
If you did not have an ego you would still care who won.
If I did not have an ego, I would never use a gun!

Ego is IS a dirty word.
You should believe what you've seen & heard.

Some people keep their egos in a bottom drawer.
Have a fridge full of Leonard Cohen.
Have to get drunk just to walk out the door.
Stay drunk to keep on goin'.
So, if you have no ego.
You don't have to keep it in good shape.
No exercise is required.
And you don't have get it down on tape!

Ego is IS a dirty word.
You better believe what you've seen & heard.

Ego is IS a dirty word.
You gotta believe what you've seen & heard.

Ego is IS a dirty word.
You must believe what you've seen & heard.

NO Ego!

"With apologies to Gregory J Macainsh (Ego is Not a Dirty Word)"

"The Don"
16.08.2020

The Girl from Ipanema Returns
(Vuelve la Chica de Ipanema)

She's been all around the world.
She's very famous, everyone knows her.
She is very beautiful.
Her beauty is well known.
She even has a song written about her.
Actually, she has quite a few songs written about her.
The one I'm thinking of is written & sung by Peter Sarstedt.
Do you know the one?
The one that begins with that haunting piano accordion intro.
I Love that song!
It's called, "Where Do You Go to (my lovely?)".

We all know where she goes.
She goes back to Ipanema.
That's her home.
That's where heart belongs.
She will travel the world.
Have friends in high places.
Stay in magnificent cites & palaces.
But she always returns to Ipanema.

This is the place where she first fell in Love.
Making Love on the beach.
The waves washing away her sins.
The moonlight glistening on her naked body.
Just like the stars up in the sky.
Some say that we can are made of star stuff.
Well, I can believe that.
Her beauty is no less than, those stars themselves.
Her hair is like the rays of light from the sun itself.
Golden & blowing in the gentle breeze like the solar flares flying out into space.

If you are ever lucky enough to meet.
To gaze your unworthy eyes on her divine splendour.
Don't walk away.
Don't look away.
Don't be shy.
Don't be nervous.
Go up to her & say "Hi".
She'll like that.

Tell her your story about your life.
Of all the times you've been rejected by Love.
Of all the times you slept be alone in your bed.
Hoping to share it with somebody else.
To hold them tight.
To feel their warmth.
To gently sway in their nakedness.
To become intoxicated by their perfume.
To spoon together until the morning comes.

She will understand.
She will feel your longing.
She will know who you are.
She will see her reflection on your eyes.
She will shed tears of happiness.
Of pure abandonment & joy.
At last she has returned.
At last she is home.
For the girl from Ipanema has returned.

"The Don"
17.08.2020

Eat My Pussy

(Mangia la Mia Figa)

Eat my pussy.
Suck on my clit.
Have some of my muff pie.
Walk into my "Tunnel of LO♥e".
Put your tongue into my "Glory Hole".
Let me cum in your mouth.
Give me a good time.
Send me to Heaven.
Make me cry with ecstasy.
Let me writhe in pure pleasure.
Let me sit on your face.
Make me bend over backwards.
Contort my body into unknown shapes.
Make me scream & shout.
Let me hang it all out.
Let me make strange faces.
Make me explode into pieces.
Don't stop until I drop.
When I've cum once, make me cum again.
Don't worry about breathing.
Think of me as a musical instrument.
Play sweet tunes with my body.
Building me up to a crescendo.
Like one of Beethoven's symphonies.
Play me like a violin.
Or like Corelli's accordion.
Keep going until you are exhausted.
Don't worry, I'll make sure you're rewarded.

"The Don"
18.08.2020

"Vulva"
Artist: "Rita B."

It's Not About What I want
(Non si Tratta di Quello che Voglio)

It's about you need.
It's about you desires.
It's about you require.
It's about you.

It's about your needs.
It's about what makes you happy.
It's about your happiness.
It's about you.

It's not about what I want.
It's not about what I need.
It's not about what I desire.
It's not about what I require.
It's not about me.

If you want it.
If you need it.
If you desire it.
If you require it
I will receive it.

It's not about me.
It's not about what I want.
It about what you want.
It's about you.

And that is that!

"The Don"
28.08.2020

Books written by "The Don"

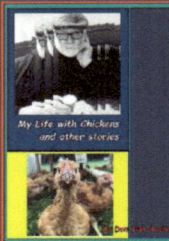
"My Life with Chickens & other stories: I Pity the Poor Immigrant"
Published:
10th September, 2019
Autobiography Book 1:
0 – 12 years old

"Poems for Misfits, Miscreants, Misanthropes, Mavericks, Losers & Malcontents!"
Published:
10th June, 2020
Book of Poems 1

"Poems for Troubled Minds & Trouble Hearts"
Published:
10th August, 2020
Book of Poems 2

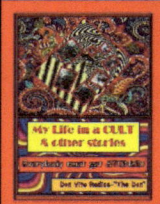
"My Life in a CULT & other stories: Everybody Must Get STONED!"
Published:
10th September, 2020
Autobiography Book 2:
15 – 30 years old

"Poems for Restless Minds & Restless Hearts"
Published:
10th October, 2020
Book of Poems 3

"Poems for Anarchists, Revolutionaries, Outlaws & Dissidents!"
Published:
10th November, 2020
Book of Poems 4

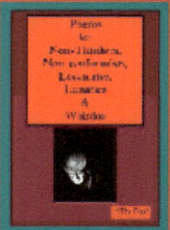
"Poems for Non-Thinkers & Eccentrics"
Published:
10th December, 2020
Book of Poems 5

"The Rantings of a Madman"
Published:
10th January, 2021
Book of Poems 6

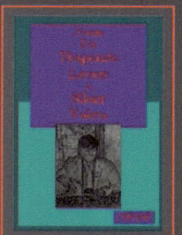
"Poems for Desperate Lovers & Silent Voices"
Published:
10th February, 2021
Book of Poems 7

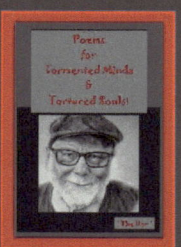
"Poems for Tormented Minds & Tortured Souls"
Published:
10th March, 2021
Book of Poems 8

All available ONLY online

Acknowledgement of Land & of the Traditional Owners of this Land

I would like to acknowledge the Gadigal people of the Eora Nation, upon whose stolen land I stand on today.

I recognise that this land was never terra nullius — the land belonging to these peoples was never ceded, given up, bought or sold.

I would like to pay my respects to Aboriginal Elders past, present and emerging, and I extend this acknowledgement to all Aboriginal and Torres Strait Islander people.

Belong

I am a life under
Moonlight, starlight and sunlight
With my Mothers earth on my feet I walk free
Through fresh and saltwater as I
Move in shallow and deep water from her womb
As little creatures so small move with such big hearts
As they take care of my Mother earth, plants and trees as I take breath
My spirit sings and dances our dreams as I know I belong here
Always was
Always will be
Our Aboriginal Land

Kathryn Dodd Farrawell
(Kaanju/Birri Widdi Woman, Cape York, North QLD & Glebe Community)
(k.farrawell@optusnet.com.au)

"Voice, Treaty, Truth"
By Kathryn Dodd Farrawell

Foreword

2020 started as strange year that continued to astonish.
In Australia, we battled bushfires, endured the floods that broke the drought, and in some places, witnessed plagues of locusts. It was biblical. But no one could be prepared for what came next. There was talk of a bad flu in China. It didn't take long for Covid-19 to reach us.

In the early days of autumn something else happened. Vito started writing poems.

It started as an sms dialogue, but the words kept coming. In many respects, Vito's poetry could be known as the "Covid Diaries'. His poems are responses and reactions to events and experiences that come to Vito in his everyday life. They have become an externalised version of what lives inside Vito's head.

His stimulus comes from all angles, as wide ranging as a Fellini movie, the taste of coffee or the look from a stranger in the street.
The poems come at all times of the night and day. Vito regularly wakes up at 3:00am with a poem in his head that has to escape. This diversity of subject matter reflects the multi-faceted diamond which is the mind of "The Don".

Mariclare Pringle
December, 2020

Detail from her quilt:
"It Depends on What Grows in Your Garden"
By Mariclaire Pringle

www.ingramcontent.com/pod-product-compliance
Lightning Source LLC
Chambersburg PA
CBHW041502010526
44107CB00049B/1620